HEALTH LAW THROUGH THE LENS OF INTERNATIONAL LAW

VOLUME 2, ISSUE 3 OF BRILLOPEDIA

ANISHA PARVIN

Copyright © Anisha Parvin
All Rights Reserved.

Contents

Preface   *v*

Author   *vii*

1. Abstract   1

2. Introduction   2

3. Historical Analysis Of Public Helath Through The Lens Of International Law   4

4. Sources Of International Health Law   6

5. The Extent Of International Health Law   8

6. Conclusion   9

Preface

"Start writing, no matter what. The water does not flow until the faucet is turned on".

• Louis L'Amour

Hundreds of students and professors are contributing their work to Brillopedia, we are here to provide ample information about Law and Contemporary issues. Our aim is to provide a platform for today's generation to express their views and ideas on law and contemporary law.

Author

Anisha Parvin

CHAPTER ONE

ABSTRACT

This paper examines the characteristics and the application of international health law, a developing area of public international law. As there is no universal international recognition of international health law as a separate branch of international law, the legal instruments relating to creating health standards are relatively fragmented. The field of international health law is still in its infancy. There are enormous obstacles to overcome, particularly in terms of improving the already available tools and addressing the obligations of non- state actors in the sphere of health. A crucial social necessity that needs to be given a louder voice at the global level is the safe guarding of health. The advancement of health related issues may be significantly aided by international law and instruments for defining international standards. This is an interest and protection of this interest must be sufficiently important. Moreover, a failure to protect this interest would be a matter of international concern.

<u>KEY WORDS</u>

International health law, society, human rights.

CHAPTER TWO

INTRODUCTION

Globalization is having major consequences not only for the world's economies, but also for the health of both populations and individuals around the world.[1] It offers a variety of significant issues to the health sector, necessitating national and international responses. Such world wide responses typically concentrate on stopping the spread of infectious illnesses.[2] Health disparities both inside and between countries are getting worse, according to public health study.[3] Changes in illness patterns , some of which are lifestyle – related , have been brought on by global trade and the expanding influence of multinational corporations.

On the other hand international health related operations carried out by nonprofit and intergovernmental organisations have largely ignored international law in the decades following WW II. The potential for international law to benefit global public health during a time when the field of international law experienced rapid expansion remained unexplored. Public opinion on international law has begun to shift in the latter half of the 1990s.[4]

During its first fifty years WHO overlooked international law. Arguments are made that WHO should fundamentally alter its approach toward international law in light of the structural and public health factors that make international law necessary, as well as WHO's historical disregard for international law. These justifications for increased WHO's involvement in international law are crucial, but they must be supported by knowledge of the role that health plays in international law.[5]

However we are all aware that , unlike international trade law, international environmental law and international humanitarian law, international health law is still in its infancy. Nevertheless , in the age of globalization , it is crucial to prioritise the protection of health more prominently in international law in order to strike a balance between the interests of trade, economic growth , and conflict and those of individual and collective health.

The New Delhi Declaration on Global Health Law was adopted by the delegates at the International Conference on Global Health Law that the WHO and the ILI sponsored in New Delhi in December 1997.

Furthermore, new WHO activities and regulations seem tobe modifying the organisation's long –standing hostility to international law. The International Health Regulations , the primary body of international law governing the prevention and control of infectious diseases,are now being updated by WHO.

Henceforth, the goal of the author in this paper is to advocate for global health protection. There is a pressing need to balance factors like global trade, industry , and commerce, as well as military objectives , against the preservation of health across the globe.

[1]Brigit Toebes, 'International Health Law: AnEmerging Field Of Public International Law' , SSRN Electronic Journal (JUNE 5, 2022 11 PM) https://www.researchgate.net/piblication/272302246

[2] Id. At 1

[3] Id. At 1

[4]Fidler , David P. " International Law and Global Public Health" (1999). Articles by Maurer Faculty.652.https:// www.repository .law. Indiana.edu/facpub/652

[5] Id. At 4

CHAPTER THREE

HISTORICAL ANALYSIS OF PUBLIC HELATH THROUGH THE LENS OF INTERNATIONAL LAW

The history of international health diplomacy from the middle of the 19th century to WWII is not reflected in WHO's approach toward international law. International law has been crucial to fostering global health co-operation ever since the inaugural International Sanitary Conference in 1851. Through this conference , disease control was elevated from a purely national problemto one that concerned the entire international community.[1]

Moreover midway through the 19[th]century , European States realized they needed to work together through international law to stop the spread of contagious diseases like Cholera and other diseases that could no longer be controlled by a state on its own.[2]

Furthermore the area in which international law was most frequently applied was the prevention of infectious diseases in people. In addition , for global health organizations were founded in the first fifty years of the 20th century. Aside from those institutions,utilizing international law for public health goals has not proven to be simple, despite the extensive list of treaties.[3]

There are numerous worldwide legal systems that uphold the value of protecting human health. Although the author has attempted to simplify such tools, it is very difficult to describe a complete legal framework where international law reflects the value of health.

[1] Id. At 4

[2]Fidler , David P. " International Law and Global Public Health" (1999). Articles by Maurer Faculty.652.https:// www.repository .law. Indiana.edu/facpub/652

[3] Id. At 7

CHAPTER FOUR

SOURCES OF INTERNATIONAL HEALTH LAW

Human Rights Law

International health law also has a significant impact on international human rights law. The right to the highest possible quality of health is the most crucial human rights principle since . International health law preserve health.

The WHO was the first organization to establish right to health. The adoption of the right to health by the WHO was a milestone in the development of international health and human rights law and served as a crucial starting point for the further development of a right to health in human rights documents.[1]

The right to health provisions that were later created, in particular Article 12 of UN International Covenant on Economic, Social and Cultural rights were influenced by the rights to health clause in the WHO Constitution. It acknowledges the right to the highest standard of health that is reasonable attainable and lists some specific action that states must take to achieve this objective.

Many other human rights, such as the right to life, the prohibition against torture and right to knowledge and education, in addition to the right to health, are in some way related to health. The emerging human rights field of health and human rights plays an important role in the international health law.

WHO's Legal document

Articles 19, 21 and 23 of the WHO Constitution, respectively, provide for the adoption of three various types of instruments, including conventions , rules and recommendations.

[1] Id .At 7

CHAPTER FIVE

THE EXTENT OF INTERNATIONAL HEALTH LAW

There has been a persistent and expanding need for international collaboration in this area due to the increasing globalization of infectious illnesses. In order to provide protection against a variety of dangers to public health, theWHO adopted a new set of international health regulation in 2005. A significant international response was not implemented, despite the fact that the domestic health systems in the afflicted countries felt to address the problem appropriately.

In terms of international health law , it is also crucial to evaluate how the regulations interact with human right standards, particularly those that relate to specific patients and those who may potentially spread the disease.

In addition , as already indicated ,international health law needs to address the links between armed conflict and health. The relationship between conflict and health has been emphasized in various occasions.

In addition to healthcare , international health law should focus on protecting the fundamental factors that influence health, access to clean water, sanitary condition and others. From the perspective of international health law the possibilities for adopting and international instrument addressing these matters could be considered.

CONCLUSION

From the foregoing discussion it is evident that the fresh thinking about international law in global public health is needed in the contemporary discourse. The idea of global health jurisprudence is intended to refocus legal thinking for the global period in perspective of global health.